D1633471

Breakfast Sandwich
Maker Cookbook

**45 Delicious, Quick and Simple
Breakfast Sandwiches You Can
Make With Your Breakfast
Sandwich Maker**

Breakfast Sandwich Maker Cookbook

Copyright © 2013 by James Heather

All rights reserved. This book or any portion thereof may not be reproduced or used in any manner whatsoever without the express written permission of the publisher except for the use of brief quotations in a book review.

Printed in the United States of America.

First Printing, 2013

Table of Contents

Introduction

What does your morning meal look like? Do you sit down for a bowl of cold cereal or simply fill a to-go mug with coffee and hop in the car? For many people, breakfast is a good idea but simply not something they have time for. In today's world, people are constantly on the go from dawn to dusk, and the busiest part of the day is often the morning.

Think for a moment what it would be like if, instead of that bowl of cold cereal, you could bite into a hot breakfast sandwich loaded with egg, ham and cheese. What if you could enjoy a customized breakfast sandwich with your favorite ingredients without wasting time at the drive-through or waiting in line at the diner down the street? If this sounds too good to be true, think again! Your breakfast dreams are about to come true thanks to the breakfast sandwich maker.

A breakfast sandwich maker is the solution to your breakfast problems and it is soon to become your favorite kitchen appliance. In this book you will learn not only about the importance of eating a good breakfast in the morning, but also about how a breakfast sandwich maker can help you start your day on the right foot. This book also includes 40+ recipes for delicious breakfast sandwiches made right in your own kitchen, whenever you want them.

Chapter One: The Importance of Breakfast

When you are running late in the morning, struggling to find your keys just to rush out the door to work, breakfast may be the last thing on your mind. Even when you are busy, however, it is never a good idea to skip breakfast. Breakfast is often referred to as the most important meal of the day, and for good reason! A healthy breakfast gives your body the nutrients and energy you need to get started on the right foot – it ensures that you are awake and focused throughout the morning and it gets your metabolism started right from the get-go.

Eating breakfast has also been shown to have benefits for weight loss. Many people mistakenly believe that skipping breakfast is a simple way to lose weight – after all, you're eliminating those calories from your daily intake, right? Wrong. Studies have shown that eating breakfast in the morning helps to reduce hunger throughout the day and helps encourage you to make healthier eating choices later on. If you skip breakfast, you are likely to be hungry and may eat more snacks and unhealthy foods throughout the day, thus negating those calories you skipped in the morning.

Breakfast is an incredibly important part of your day, but it doesn't have to become a chore or something else to add to your "to do" list. There are a number of ways to make eating breakfast both fun and fast. One great example is the breakfast sandwich maker! This device takes all of your favorite breakfast foods like bagels, eggs, ham and cheese and combines them into a delicious breakfast sandwich in just a few minutes. A breakfast sandwich maker is the perfect solution for busy professionals and families, as well as college students and anyone who has limited time in the morning.

Keep reading to learn more about these wonderful devices and to receive more than 40 delicious breakfast sandwich recipes designed for breakfast sandwich makers!

Chapter Two: The Low-Down on Breakfast Sandwich Makers

Before you get into breakfast sandwich maker recipes, you should learn the basics about this wonderful appliance. A breakfast sandwich maker is a type of electric kitchen appliance that serves the sole purpose of cooking single-serving sandwiches in 5 minutes or less. These devices are easy to use, easy to clean, and will transform the way you eat breakfast. Below you will find a list of some of the benefits of a breakfast sandwich maker:

Benefits of breakfast sandwich makers include:

- All-in-one device, makes breakfast convenient

Breakfast Sandwich Maker Cookbook

- Creates perfect single-serving breakfast sandwiches with little prep

- Cooks a variety of recipes in 5 minutes or less

- Easy to disassemble and clean – inserts are typically dishwasher safe

- Saves money on buying breakfast out each morning

- Sandwiches are easy to take on the go, even to school or work

- Egg cooks to perfection – won't be soggy or slide out between slices of bread

- Breakfast meats are reheated to the right temperature

- Sandwich stays together when you eat it – no mess and little clean-up

Now that you know the benefits of a breakfast sandwich maker, you may be curious about the details. What does it look like and how does it work? A breakfast sandwich maker is a small, rounded appliance that opens on a hinge. There is typically a rounded metal mold attached to both the top and bottom halves of the appliance that come together to contain and cook the sandwich when the sandwich maker is closed. This feature ensures that the sandwich is fully contained for the ideal shape and that all of the ingredients are warmed to perfection.

Perhaps the most unique feature of a breakfast sandwich maker, however, is the round flat tray that can be rotated in an out of the machine by hand to separate and cook raw egg. After placing the bread, cheese and other ingredients in the bottom of the mold, you slide the egg tray into place and add the egg. You then top the egg with the second piece of bread and close the sandwich maker to let it cook. In about 5 minutes' time, you rotate the egg cooking tray out of the sandwich maker, bringing all of the layers of the sandwich together. Simply open the appliance, then, and remove your completed breakfast sandwich!

If you have large sized croissants, French toast, square waffles etc. you can, if you wish, use a large round cookie cutter to trim them down to the right size to fit the sandwich maker.

As a side note: please ensure that when using any kind of meat, that it's precooked before being used in a sandwich maker. The sandwich maker only reheats precooked meat.

Chapter Three: Breakfast Sandwich Maker Recipes

BREAKFAST RECIPES

Classic Egg, Ham and Cheese

Sausage and Cheese

Easy Ham and Scrambled Egg

Avocado, Swiss and Bacon

Spinach, Parmesan and Egg White

Traditional BLT

Waffle, Egg and Sausage

Bacon Cheddar Croissant

Meat Lover's Biscuit

Egg Whites with Mozzarella

Hash Brown Sausage Sandwich

Monte Cristo Sandwich

Canadian Bacon Bagel Sandwich

Donut Breakfast Sandwich

Eggs Benedict with Ham

Classic Egg, Ham and Cheese

Serves 1

Prep Time: 5 minutes

Cook Time: 5 minutes

Nutritional Value: 300 calories, 28g carbs, 12g fat, 20g protein

Ingredients:

1 toasted English muffin, sliced

2 slices deli ham

1 slice cheddar cheese

1 large egg

Instructions:

1. Preheat the breakfast sandwich maker.

2. Place half of the English muffin, cut-side up, inside the bottom tray of the sandwich maker.

3. Fold the slices of ham on top of the English muffin half and top with the slice of cheddar cheese.

4. Slide the egg tray into place and crack the egg into it.

5. Top the egg with the other half of the English muffin.

6. Close the sandwich maker and cook for 4 to 5 minutes until the egg is cooked through.

7. Carefully rotate the egg tray out of the sandwich maker then open the sandwich maker and enjoy your sandwich.

Sausage and Cheese

Serves 1

Prep Time: 5 minutes

Cook Time: 5 minutes

Nutritional Value: 405 calories, 26g carbs, 31g fat, 20g protein

Ingredients:

1 buttermilk biscuit, sliced

1 maple pork sausage patty, cooked

1 slice cheddar cheese

1 large egg, beaten

Instructions:

1. Preheat the breakfast sandwich maker.

2. Place half of the biscuit, cut-side up, inside the bottom tray of the sandwich maker.

3. Arrange the sausage patty on top of the biscuit and top with the slice of cheddar cheese.

4. Slide the egg tray into place and pour the beaten egg into it.

5. Top the egg with the other half of the biscuit.

6. Close the sandwich maker and cook for 4 to 5 minutes until the egg is cooked through.

7. Carefully rotate the egg tray out of the sandwich maker then open the sandwich maker and enjoy your sandwich.

Easy Ham and Scrambled Egg

Serves 1

Prep Time: 5 minutes

Cook Time: 5 minutes

Nutritional Value: 330 calories, 26g carbs, 14g fat, 22g protein

Ingredients:

2 slices whole grain bread

2 slices deli ham

1 slice Swiss cheese

1 large egg

2 teaspoons heavy cream

1 teaspoon chopped chives

Instructions:

1. Preheat the breakfast sandwich maker.

2. Place one slice of bread in the bottom tray of the sandwich maker.

3. Arrange the slices of ham on top of the bread and top with the slice of Swiss cheese.

4. Beat together the egg, heavy cream and chives in a small bowl.

5. Slide the egg tray into place over the cheese and pour the beaten egg mixture into the tray.

6. Top the egg mixture with the remaining slice of bread.

7. Close the sandwich maker and cook for 4 to 5 minutes until the egg is cooked through.

8. Carefully rotate the egg tray out of the sandwich maker then open the sandwich maker and enjoy your sandwich.

Avocado, Swiss and Bacon

Serves 1

Prep Time: 5 minutes

Cook Time: 5 minutes

Nutritional Value: 570 calories, 37g carbs, 38g fat, 26g protein

Ingredients:

1 croissant, sliced

2 slices bacon, cooked

1 slice Swiss cheese

¼ avocado, pitted and sliced

1 large egg

1 tablespoon basil pesto

Instructions:

1. Divide the pesto between the two halves of the croissant, spreading it evenly.
2. Preheat the breakfast sandwich maker.
3. Place half of the croissant, pesto-side up, inside the bottom tray of the sandwich maker.
4. Arrange the slices of bacon on top of the bagel and top with the slice of Swiss cheese.
5. Slide the egg tray into place and crack the egg into it.
6. Top the egg with the other half of the croissant, pesto-side down.
7. Close the sandwich maker and cook for 4 to 5 minutes until the egg is cooked through.
8. Carefully rotate the egg tray out of the sandwich maker then open the sandwich maker and enjoy your sandwich.

Spinach, Parmesan and Egg White

Serves 1

Prep Time: 5 minutes

Cook Time: 5 minutes

Nutritional Value: 200 calories, 31g carbs, 3g fat, 14g protein

Ingredients:

1 toasted English muffin, sliced

½ cup baby spinach leaves

2 large egg whites

1 tablespoon grated parmesan cheese

1 clove garlic, minced

Instructions:

1. Preheat the breakfast sandwich maker.

2. Place half of the English muffin, cut-side up, inside the bottom tray of the sandwich maker.

3. Arrange the baby spinach leaves on top of the English muffin.

4. Beat the egg whites, parmesan cheese and garlic in a small bowl.

5. Slide the egg tray into place and pour the egg mixture into it.

6. Top the egg with the other half of the English muffin.

7. Close the sandwich maker and cook for 4 to 5 minutes until the egg is cooked through.

8. Carefully rotate the egg tray out of the sandwich maker then open the sandwich maker and enjoy your sandwich.

Traditional BLT

Serves 1

Prep Time: 5 minutes

Cook Time: 5 minutes

Nutritional Value: 290 calories, 28g carbs, 16g fat, 13g protein

Ingredients:

2 slices white bread

3 slices bacon, cooked

2 thin slices tomato

1 leaf Romaine lettuce, torn in half

2 teaspoons mayonnaise

Instructions:

1. Spread one teaspoon of mayonnaise on each slice of bread.
2. Preheat the breakfast sandwich maker.

3. Place one slice of bread inside the bottom tray of the sandwich maker, mayonnaise-side facing up.

4. Break the slices of bacon in half and place them on top of the bread. Top with the slices of tomato.

5. Top the sandwich with the other slice of bread, mayonnaise-side down.

6. Close the sandwich maker and cook for 4 to 5 minutes.

7. Carefully open the sandwich maker and remove the top slice of bread.

8. Add the lettuce then replace the bread and enjoy your sandwich.

Waffle, Egg and Sausage

Serves 1

Prep Time: 5 minutes

Cook Time: 5 minutes

Nutritional Value: 430 calories, 31g carbs, 28g fat, 18g protein

Ingredients:

2 round frozen waffles

1 pork sausage patty, cooked

1 large egg

1 teaspoon maple syrup

Instructions:

1. Preheat the breakfast sandwich maker.
2. Place one of the waffles inside the bottom tray of the sandwich maker.

3. Put the sausage patty on top of the waffle.

4. Slide the egg tray into place and crack the egg into it.

5. Top the egg with the other waffle.

6. Close the sandwich maker and cook for 4 to 5 minutes until the egg is cooked through.

7. Carefully rotate the egg tray out of the sandwich maker then open the sandwich maker.

8. Remove the top waffle and drizzle the egg with maple syrup.

9. Replace the waffle and enjoy your sandwich.

Bacon Cheddar Croissant

Serves 1

Prep Time: 5 minutes

Cook Time: 5 minutes

Nutritional Value: 520 calories, 22g carbs, 32g fat, 24g protein

Ingredients:

1 croissant, sliced

2 slices bacon, cooked

1 slice cheddar cheese

1 large egg, beaten

Instructions:

1. Preheat the breakfast sandwich maker.
2. Place half of the croissant, cut-side up, inside the bottom tray of the sandwich maker.

3. Break the slices of bacon in half and arrange them on top of the croissant then top with the slice of cheddar cheese.

4. Slide the egg tray into place and pour the beaten egg into it.

5. Top the egg with the other half of the croissant.

6. Close the sandwich maker and cook for 4 to 5 minutes until the egg is cooked through.

7. Carefully rotate the egg tray out of the sandwich maker then open the sandwich maker and enjoy your sandwich.

Meat Lover's Biscuit

Serves 1

Prep Time: 5 minutes

Cook Time: 5 minutes

Nutritional Value: 390 calories, 30g carbs, 17g fat, 30g protein

Ingredients:

1 buttermilk biscuit, sliced

2 slices Canadian bacon

1 pork sausage patty, cooked

1 slice deli ham

1 large egg

Instructions:

1. Preheat the breakfast sandwich maker.
2. Place half of the biscuit, cut-side up, inside the bottom tray of the sandwich maker.

3. Arrange the slices of Canadian bacon, sausage and ham on top of the biscuit half.

4. Slide the egg tray into place and crack the egg into it.

5. Top the egg with the other half of the biscuit.

6. Close the sandwich maker and cook for 4 to 5 minutes until the egg is cooked through.

7. Carefully rotate the egg tray out of the sandwich maker then open the sandwich maker and enjoy your sandwich.

Egg Whites with Mozzarella

Serves 1

Prep Time: 5 minutes

Cook Time: 5 minutes

Nutritional Value: 210 calories, 27g carbs, 6g fat, 18g protein

Ingredients:

1 thin sandwich bun, sliced

1 thick slice tomato

1 slice mozzarella cheese

2 large egg whites, beaten

Instructions:

1. Preheat the breakfast sandwich maker.
2. Place half of the sandwich bun, cut-side up, inside the bottom tray of the sandwich maker.

3. Arrange the slices of tomato and mozzarella cheese over the sandwich bun.

4. Slide the egg tray into place and crack the egg into it.

5. Top the egg with the other half of the sandwich bun.

6. Close the sandwich maker and cook for 4 to 5 minutes until the egg is cooked through.

7. Carefully rotate the egg tray out of the sandwich maker then open the sandwich maker and enjoy your sandwich.

Hash Brown Sausage Sandwich

Serves 1

Prep Time: 10 minutes

Cook Time: 5 minutes

Nutritional Value: 620 calories, 37g carbs, 48g fat, 19g protein

Ingredients:

2 frozen hash brown patties

1 turkey sausage patty

1 slice cheddar cheese

1 large egg, beaten

Instructions:

1. Heat the butter in a small skillet over medium heat. Add the hash brown patties and cook until lightly browned on one side.

2. Flip the patties and cook until browned on the other side.

3. Preheat the breakfast sandwich maker.

4. Place one of the hash brown patties inside the bottom ring of the sandwich maker.

5. Top the hash brown with the sausage patty and slice of cheddar cheese.

6. Slide the egg tray into place and crack the egg into it.

7. Top the egg with the other hash brown patty.

8. Close the sandwich maker and cook for 4 to 5 minutes until the egg is cooked through.

9. Carefully rotate the egg tray out of the sandwich maker then open the sandwich maker and enjoy your sandwich.

Monte Cristo Sandwich

Serves 1

Prep Time: 5 minutes

Cook Time: 5 minutes

Nutritional Value: 400 calories, 40g carbs, 17g fat, 21g protein

Ingredients:

2 slices frozen French toast

1 slice deli ham

1 slice provolone cheese

1 slice Swiss cheese

1 teaspoon maple syrup

Instructions:

1. Preheat the breakfast sandwich maker.
2. Place one slice of French toast inside the bottom tray of the sandwich maker.

3. Arrange the slices of ham, provolone and Swiss cheese on top of the French toast slice.

4. Lower the ring on the top of the breakfast sandwich maker into place and place the other slice of French toast on top of the cheese.

5. Close the sandwich maker and cook for 4 to 5 minutes until the cheese is melted and the French toast heated through.

6. Carefully open the sandwich maker and drizzle the sandwich with maple syrup to enjoy.

Canadian Bacon Bagel Sandwich

Serves 1

Prep Time: 5 minutes

Cook Time: 5 minutes

Nutritional Value: 480 calories, 58g carbs, 17g fat, 28g protein

Ingredients:

1 sesame seed bagel, cut in half

2 slices Canadian bacon

1 slice cheddar cheese

1 large egg

Instructions:

1. Preheat the breakfast sandwich maker.
2. Place half of the bagel, cut-side up, inside the bottom tray of the sandwich maker.

3. Arrange the slices of Canadian bacon on top of the bagel and top with the slice of cheddar cheese.

4. Slide the egg tray into place and crack the egg into it.

5. Top the egg with the other half of the bagel.

6. Close the sandwich maker and cook for 4 to 5 minutes until the egg is cooked through.

7. Carefully rotate the egg tray out of the sandwich maker then open the sandwich maker and enjoy your sandwich.

Donut Breakfast Sandwich

Serves 1

Prep Time: 5 minutes

Cook Time: 5 minutes

Nutritional Value: 460 calories, 25g carbs, 31g fat, 20g protein

Ingredients:

1 glazed donut, cut in half

2 slices cooked bacon

1 slice provolone cheese

1 large egg

Instructions:

1. Preheat the breakfast sandwich maker.
2. Place half of the donut, cut-side up, inside the bottom tray of the sandwich maker.

3. Cut or break the bacon slices in half and place them on top of the donut half. Top with the slice of provolone cheese.

4. Slide the egg tray into place and crack the egg into it.

5. Top the egg with the other half of the donut.

6. Close the sandwich maker and cook for 4 to 5 minutes until the egg is cooked through.

7. Carefully rotate the egg tray out of the sandwich maker then open the sandwich maker and enjoy your sandwich.

Eggs Benedict with Ham

Serves 1

Prep Time: 10 minutes

Cook Time: 5 minutes

Nutritional Value: 860 calories, 51g carbs, 64g fat, 27g protein

Ingredients:

4 tablespoons unsalted butter

1 large egg yolk

2 teaspoons lemon juice

Pinch cayenne pepper

Pinch salt

1 whole wheat bagel, sliced

½ cup fresh spinach leaves

2 slices cooked bacon

1 large egg, beaten

Instructions:

1. Preheat the breakfast sandwich maker.
2. Melt the butter in a small saucepan over medium heat.
3. Blend the egg yolks, lemon juice, cayenne and salt in a blender then drizzle into the saucepan.
4. Cook for 10 seconds, stirring well, then remove from heat and set aside.
5. Place half of the bagel, cut-side up, inside the bottom tray of the sandwich maker.
6. Top the bagel half with spinach leaves. Break the bacon slices in half and place them on top of the spinach.
7. Slide the egg tray into place and pour the beaten egg into it.
8. Top the egg with the other half of the bagel.

9. Close the sandwich maker and cook for 4 to 5 minutes until the egg is cooked through.

10. Carefully rotate the egg tray out of the sandwich maker then open the sandwich maker.

11. Take the top bagel off the sandwich and drizzle the eggs with the hollandaise sauce.

12. Replace the bagel half and enjoy your sandwich.

VEGETARIAN BREAKFAST RECIPES

Egg and Cheddar Cheese Biscuit

Creamy Brie Pancake Sandwich

Tomato, Egg and Avocado

Italian Egg Whites on Ciabatta

Portabella Mushroom Sandwich

Margherita Flatbread Mini

Fried Egg and Cheese Bagel

Muffuletta Breakfast Sandwich

Eggs Florentine Biscuit

Cinnamon Raisin Apple Sandwich

Egg and Cheddar Cheese Biscuit

Serves 1

Prep Time: 5 minutes

Cook Time: 5 minutes

Nutritional Value: 320 calories, 29g carbs, 17g fat, 14g protein

Ingredients:

1 biscuit, sliced

1 slice cheddar cheese

1 slice red onion

1 slice green pepper, seeded and cored

1 large egg

Instructions:

1. Preheat the breakfast sandwich maker.

2. Place half of the biscuit, cut-side up, inside the bottom tray of the sandwich maker.

3. Top the biscuit with a slice of cheddar cheese along with the red onion and green pepper.

4. Slide the egg tray into place and crack the egg into it.

5. Top the egg with the other half of the biscuit.

6. Close the sandwich maker and cook for 4 to 5 minutes until the egg is cooked through.

7. Carefully rotate the egg tray out of the sandwich maker then open the sandwich maker and enjoy your sandwich.

Creamy Brie Pancake Sandwich

Serves 1

Prep Time: 5 minutes

Cook Time: 5 minutes

Nutritional Value: 410 calories, 43g carbs, 20g fat, 15g protein

Ingredients:

2 frozen pancakes

1 tablespoon raspberry jam

1 ounce Brie, chopped

1 large egg

Instructions:

1. Preheat the breakfast sandwich maker.
2. Place one of the pancakes inside the bottom tray of the sandwich maker and spread the raspberry jam on top.

3. Sprinkle the chopped brie on top of the pancake.

4. Slide the egg tray into place and crack the egg into it.

5. Top the egg with the other pancake.

6. Close the sandwich maker and cook for 4 to 5 minutes until the egg is cooked through.

7. Carefully rotate the egg tray out of the sandwich maker then open the sandwich maker and enjoy your sandwich.

Tomato, Egg and Avocado

Serves 1

Prep Time: 5 minutes

Cook Time: 5 minutes

Nutritional Value: 540 calories, 45g carbs, 32g fat, 19g protein

Ingredients:

1 croissant, sliced

2 slices ripe tomato

¼ ripe avocado, pitted and sliced

1 slice Swiss cheese

1 large egg

1 tablespoon sliced green onion

2 teaspoons half-n-half

Instructions:

1. Preheat the breakfast sandwich maker.
2. Place half of the croissant, cut-side up, inside the bottom tray of the sandwich maker.
3. Top the croissant with the tomato and avocado, then top with the slice of Swiss cheese.
4. Whisk together the egg, green onion and half-n-half in a small bowl.
5. Slide the egg tray into place and pour the egg mixture into it.
6. Top the egg with the other half of the croissant.
7. Close the sandwich maker and cook for 4 to 5 minutes until the egg is cooked through.
8. Carefully rotate the egg tray out of the sandwich maker then open the sandwich maker and enjoy your sandwich.

Italian Egg Whites on Ciabatta

Serves 1

Prep Time: 5 minutes

Cook Time: 5 minutes

Nutritional Value: 330 calories, 46g carbs, 12g fat, 22g protein

Ingredients:

1 ciabatta sandwich roll, sliced

1 teaspoon unsalted butter

1 slice mozzarella cheese

2 large egg whites

1 tablespoon skim milk

1 clove garlic, minced

1 teaspoon chopped chives

1/8 teaspoon dried Italian seasoning

Instructions:

1. Preheat the breakfast sandwich maker.
2. Place half of ciabatta roll, cut-side up, inside the bottom tray of the sandwich maker.
3. Spread the butter on the ciabatta roll. Top with the slice of mozzarella cheese.
4. Whisk together the egg whites, milk, garlic, chives and Italian seasoning.
5. Slide the egg tray into place and pour the egg mixture into it.
6. Top the egg with the other half of the ciabatta roll.
7. Close the sandwich maker and cook for 4 to 5 minutes until the egg is cooked through.
8. Carefully rotate the egg tray out of the sandwich maker then open the sandwich maker and enjoy your sandwich.

Portabella Mushroom Sandwich

Serves 1

Prep Time: 5 minutes

Cook Time: 5 minutes

Nutritional Value: 370 calories, 33g carbs, 17g fat, 18g protein

Ingredients:

1 whole wheat English muffin, sliced

1 teaspoon olive oil

1 portabella mushroom cap

1 slice provolone cheese

1 large egg

½ cup spring greens

Instructions:

1. Brush the English muffin with olive oil.

2. Preheat the breakfast sandwich maker.

3. Place half of the English muffin, cut-side up, inside the bottom tray of the sandwich maker.

4. Put the mushroom cap on top of the English muffin.

5. Top the mushroom cap with the slice of provolone cheese.

6. Slide the egg tray into place and crack the egg into it.

7. Top the egg with the other half of the English muffin.

8. Close the sandwich maker and cook for 4 to 5 minutes until the egg is cooked through.

9. Carefully rotate the egg tray out of the sandwich maker then open the sandwich maker.

10. Remove the top English muffin half and top the sandwich with the spring greens.
11. Replace the English muffin on top and enjoy your sandwich.

Margherita Flatbread Mini

Serves 1

Prep Time: 5 minutes

Cook Time: 5 minutes

Nutritional Value: 310 calories, 23g carbs, 19g fat, 22g protein

Ingredients:

1 round flatbread

1 teaspoon olive oil

1 clove garlic, minced

1 slice mozzarella cheese

2 thin slices ripe tomato

1 thin slice red onion

4 fresh basil leaves

Pinch dried oregano

1 large egg, beaten

2 teaspoons grated parmesan cheese

Instructions:

1. Preheat the breakfast sandwich maker.
2. Place the flatbread inside the bottom tray of the sandwich maker.
3. Brush the flatbread with the olive oil and sprinkle with garlic.
4. Add the tomatoes, red onion and basil leaves then sprinkle with dried oregano.
5. Top the vegetables with the mozzarella cheese.
6. Slide the egg tray into place and pour the beaten egg into it.
7. Close the sandwich maker and cook for 4 to 5 minutes until the egg is cooked through.
8. Carefully rotate the egg tray out of the sandwich maker then open the sandwich maker.
9. Sprinkle the sandwich with parmesan cheese then enjoy.

Fried Egg and Cheese Bagel

Serves 1

Prep Time: 5 minutes

Cook Time: 5 minutes

Nutritional Value: 430 calories, 56g carbs, 14g fat, 20g protein

Ingredients:

1 poppy seed bagel, sliced

1 ounce goat cheese

1 large egg

1 teaspoon chopped chives

Salt and pepper to taste

Instructions:

1. Preheat the breakfast sandwich maker.

2. Place half of the bagel, cut-side up, inside the bottom tray of the sandwich maker.

3. Layer the goat cheese on top of the bagel.

4. Slide the egg tray into place and crack the egg into it.

5. Sprinkle the egg with chopped chives, salt and pepper.

6. Top the egg with the other half of the bagel.

7. Close the sandwich maker and cook for 4 to 5 minutes until the egg is cooked through.

8. Carefully rotate the egg tray out of the sandwich maker then open the sandwich maker and enjoy your sandwich.

Muffuletta Breakfast Sandwich

Serves 1

Prep Time: 10 minutes

Cook Time: 5 minutes

Nutritional Value: 440 calories, 35g carbs, 19g fat, 27g protein

Ingredients:

2 slices thick white bread

1 slice deli ham

1 slice hard salami

1 slice provolone cheese

1 tbsp. chopped black olives

1 tbsp. roasted red pepper, chopped

1 teaspoon minced red onion

1 clove garlic, minced

Salt and pepper to taste

1 large egg

Instructions:

1. Stir together the olives, red pepper, red onion and garlic. Season with salt and pepper and stir well.

2. Preheat the breakfast sandwich maker.

3. Place one slice of bread inside the bottom tray of the sandwich maker.

4. Layer the ham and salami over the bread and top with the olive mixture.

5. Top the olive mixture with the slice of provolone cheese.

6. Slide the egg tray into place and crack the egg into it. Stir the egg gently to break the yolk.

7. Top the egg with the other piece of bread.

8. Close the sandwich maker and cook for 4 to 5 minutes until the egg is cooked through.

9. Carefully rotate the egg tray out of the sandwich maker then open the

sandwich maker and enjoy your
sandwich.

Eggs Florentine Biscuit

Serves 1

Prep Time: 5 minutes

Cook Time: 5 minutes

Nutritional Value: 180 calories, 11g carbs, 11g fat, 12g protein

Ingredients:

1 slice multigrain bread

1 large egg

2 tbsp. plain nonfat yogurt

¼ tsp. Dijon mustard

½ cup baby spinach

1 tbsp. minced yellow onion

1 tsp. olive oil

Instructions:

1. Heat the oil in a small skillet over medium heat. Add the onion and spinach and stir well.
2. Cook for 2 minutes, stirring, until the spinach is just wilted. Set aside.
3. Preheat the breakfast sandwich maker.
4. Place the piece of bread inside the bottom tray of the sandwich maker.
5. Whisk together the yogurt and mustard in a small bowl then brush over the piece of bread.
6. Top the bread with the cooked spinach and onion mixture.
7. Slide the egg tray into place and crack the egg into it. Use a fork to stir the egg, just breaking the yolk.
8. Close the sandwich maker and cook for 4 to 5 minutes until the egg is cooked through.

9. Carefully rotate the egg tray out of the sandwich maker then open the sandwich maker and enjoy your sandwich.

Cinnamon Raisin Apple Sandwich

Serves 1

Prep Time: 5 minutes

Cook Time: 5 minutes

Nutritional Value: 300 calories, 40g carbs, 12g fat, 9g protein

Ingredients:

2 slices cinnamon raisin bread

½ small apple, sliced thin

1 thin slice cheddar cheese

½ teaspoon unsalted butter

Pinch ground cinnamon and nutmeg

Instructions:

1. Preheat the breakfast sandwich maker.

2. Place one slice of bread inside the bottom tray of the sandwich maker. Spread the bread with butter.

3. Top the bread with the slices of apple then sprinkle them with cinnamon and nutmeg.

4. Place the slice of cheddar cheese over the apples. Top the cheese with the other piece of bread.

5. Close the sandwich maker and cook for 4 to 5 minutes until it is heated through.

6. Carefully open the sandwich maker and enjoy your sandwich.

OTHER SANDWICH RECIPES

Chipotle Chicken Sandwich

Quick and Easy Quesadillas

BLTA (Bacon, Lettuce, Tomato and Avocado)

Pepper Jack Sausage Sandwich

Smoked Salmon and Brie Sandwich

Easy Bread Pudding Sandwich

Ricotta Basil Biscuit with Nectarines

Chocolate Raspberry Croissant

Peanut Butter Banana Sandwich

Mediterranean English Muffin

Mexican-Style Egg and Beans Sandwich

Vegan Sausage Sandwich

Portabella and Spinach Croissant

Red Pepper and Goat Cheese Sandwich

Bagel with Lox Sandwich

Parmesan and Bacon on Whole Wheat

Chocolate Donut Dessert Sandwich

Tomato Basil Flatbread

Vegetarian Boca Sandwich

Cheddar Hash Brown Biscuit

Chipotle Chicken Sandwich

Serves 1

Prep Time: 5 minutes

Cook Time: 5 minutes

Nutritional Value: 560 calories, 23g carbs, 42g fat, 23g protein

Ingredients:

1 ciabatta roll, sliced

1 cooked chicken patty

1 slice Pepper Jack cheese

1 tbsp. chipotle mayonnaise

1 large egg

1 slice red onion

1 piece romaine lettuce, torn in half

Instructions:

1. Preheat the breakfast sandwich maker.
2. Place half of the ciabatta roll, cut-side up, inside the bottom tray of the sandwich maker.
3. Top the ciabatta with the chicken patty and Pepper Jack cheese.
4. Slide the egg tray into place and crack the egg into it. Use a fork to stir the egg, just breaking the yolk.
5. Brush the other half of the ciabatta roll with the chipotle mayonnaise.
6. Place the second half of the ciabatta on top of the egg.
7. Close the sandwich maker and cook for 4 to 5 minutes until the egg is cooked through.
8. Carefully rotate the egg tray out of the sandwich maker then open the sandwich maker.

9. Remove the top ciabatta roll and top the sandwich with the onion and lettuce. Replace the roll to enjoy the sandwich.

Quick and Easy Quesadillas

Serves 1

Prep Time: 10 minutes

Cook Time: 5 minutes

Nutritional Value: 400 calories, 24g carbs, 24g fat, 23g protein

Ingredients:

2 small round tortillas

2 slices cooked bacon

1 ounce shredded cheddar jack cheese

1 tbsp. minced red onion

1 tbsp. minced red pepper

1 tbsp. BBQ sauce

1 large egg

1 tbsp. fresh salsa

1 tbsp. sour cream

Instructions:

1. Preheat the breakfast sandwich maker.
2. Place one of the tortillas inside the bottom tray of the sandwich maker. Brush with BBQ sauce.
3. Break the pieces of bacon in half and place them on top of the tortilla. Sprinkle with cheese, red onion and red pepper.
4. Slide the egg tray into place and crack the egg into it. Use a fork to stir the egg, just breaking the yolk.
5. Place the second tortilla on top of the egg.
6. Close the sandwich maker and cook for 4 to 5 minutes until the egg is cooked through.
7. Carefully rotate the egg tray out of the sandwich maker then open the sandwich maker.

8. Remove the top tortilla and spread with salsa and sour cream. Replace the tortilla and enjoy your sandwich.

BLTA (Bacon, Lettuce, Tomato and Avocado)

Serves 1

Prep Time: 5 minutes

Cook Time: 5 minutes

Nutritional Value: 540 calories, 22g carbs, 41g fat, 21g protein

Ingredients:

1 croissant, sliced in half

1 tablespoon mayonnaise

Salt and pepper to taste

3 slices bacon, cooked

¼ ripe avocado, pitted and sliced

1 thick slice tomato

1 piece Romaine lettuce, torn in half

1 large egg

Instructions:

1. Preheat the breakfast sandwich maker.
2. Place half of the croissant, cut-side up, inside the bottom tray of the sandwich maker.
3. Brush the croissant with the mayonnaise and sprinkle with salt and pepper.
4. Break the bacon slices in half and arrange them on top of the croissant. Top with avocado and tomato.
5. Slide the egg tray into place and crack the egg into it. Use a fork to stir the egg, just breaking the yolk.
6. Place the second half of the croissant on top of the egg.
7. Close the sandwich maker and cook for 4 to 5 minutes until the egg is cooked through.
8. Carefully rotate the egg tray out of the sandwich maker then open the sandwich maker.

9. Remove the top of the croissant and top with the lettuce.

10. Replace the top half of the croissant then enjoy your sandwich.

Pepper Jack Sausage Sandwich

Serves 1

Prep Time: 5 minutes

Cook Time: 5 minutes

Nutritional Value: 485 calories, 26g carbs, 33g fat, 20g protein

Ingredients:

1 buttermilk biscuit, sliced in half

1 tsp. horseradish sauce

1 pork sausage patty, cooked

1 slice Pepper Jack cheese

1 large egg, beaten

Instructions:

1. Spread the horseradish sauce on the bottom half of the biscuit.
2. Preheat the breakfast sandwich maker.

3. Place the bottom half of the biscuit, cut-side up, inside the bottom tray of the sandwich maker.

4. Top the biscuit with the sausage patty and Pepper Jack cheese.

5. Slide the egg tray into place and pour the beaten egg into it.

6. Place the second half of the biscuit on top of the egg.

7. Close the sandwich maker and cook for 4 to 5 minutes until the egg is cooked through.

8. Carefully rotate the egg tray out of the sandwich maker then open the sandwich maker to enjoy your sandwich.

Smoked Salmon and Brie Sandwich

Serves 1

Prep Time: 5 minutes

Cook Time: 5 minutes

Nutritional Value: 365 calories, 23g carbs, 17g fat, 25g protein

Ingredients:

1 whole wheat English muffin, sliced

2 ounces smoked salmon

1 ounce Brie cheese, chopped

1 tbsp. chopped chives

½ tsp. chopped capers

1 large egg

Instructions:

1. Preheat the breakfast sandwich maker.

2. Place half of the English muffin, cut-side up, inside the bottom tray of the sandwich maker.

3. Top the muffin with the salmon, chopped brie, chives and capers.

4. Slide the egg tray into place and crack the egg into it. Use a fork to stir the egg, just breaking the yolk.

5. Place the second half of the English muffin on top of the egg. Close the sandwich maker and cook for 4 to 5 minutes until the egg is cooked through

6. .Carefully rotate the egg tray out of the sandwich maker then open the sandwich maker to enjoy your sandwich

Easy Bread Pudding Sandwich

Serves 1

Prep Time: 10 minutes

Cook Time: 5 minutes

Nutritional Value: 680 calories, 54g carbs, 37g fat, 34g protein

Ingredients:

2 slices stale bread, cubed

1 large egg

2 tbsp. maple syrup or honey

2 tbsp. plain yogurt

1 tbsp. melted butter

Pinch ground nutmeg

1 chicken sausage patty, cooked

1 slice Swiss cheese

1 large egg

Instructions:

1. Arrange the chunks of bread in a small round ramekin.
2. Whisk together the remaining ingredients and pour over the bread – do not stir.
3. Microwave the ramekin on high heat for 2 minutes until the pudding is firm and hot. Let cool for 5 minutes.
4. Preheat the breakfast sandwich maker.
5. Turn the bread pudding out of the ramekin and into the bottom of the breakfast sandwich maker.
6. Top the bread pudding with the sausage patty and slice of Swiss cheese.
7. Slide the egg tray into place and crack the egg into it. Use a fork to stir the egg, just breaking the yolk.
8. Close the sandwich maker and cook for 4 to 5 minutes until the egg is cooked through.

9. Carefully rotate the egg tray out of the sandwich maker then open the sandwich maker to enjoy your sandwich.

Ricotta Basil Biscuit with Nectarines

Serves 1

Prep Time: 5 minutes

Cook Time: 5 minutes

Nutritional Value: 340 calories, 55g carbs, 8g fat, 6g protein

Ingredients:

1 buttermilk biscuit, sliced

1 ripe nectarine, peeled and sliced

1 tbsp. ricotta cheese

1 tbsp. maple syrup

2 tsp. brown sugar

Instructions:

1. Place the nectarines in a bowl and add the ricotta, maple syrup and brown sugar then toss well.

2. Preheat the breakfast sandwich maker.

3. Place half of the biscuit, cut-side up, inside the bottom tray of the sandwich maker.

4. Top the muffin with the nectarine slices, ricotta, maple syrup and brown sugar mixture

5. Place the second half of the biscuit on top of the nectarines.

6. Close the sandwich maker and cook for 4 to 5 minutes until heated through.

7. Carefully open the sandwich maker and enjoy your sandwich.

Chocolate Raspberry Croissant

Serves 1

Prep Time: 5 minutes

Cook Time: 5 minutes

Nutritional Value: 515 calories, 49g carbs, 31g fat, 10g protein

Ingredients:

1 croissant, sliced

2 tbsp. chocolate hazelnut spread

½ cup fresh raspberries

2 tbsp. crème fraiche

Instructions:

1. Brush 1 tbsp. chocolate hazelnut spread on each half of the croissant.
2. Preheat the breakfast sandwich maker.

3. Place half of the croissant, cut-side up, inside the bottom tray of the sandwich maker.

4. Top the croissant with the raspberries and crème fraiche.

5. Place the second half of the croissant on top of the raspberries.

6. Close the sandwich maker and cook for 4 to 5 minutes until heated through.

7. Carefully open the sandwich maker and enjoy your sandwich.

Peanut Butter Banana Sandwich

Serves 1

Prep Time: 5 minutes

Cook Time: 5 minutes

Nutritional Value: 430 calories, 23g carbs, 1g fat, 1g protein

Ingredients:

2 slices white bread

2 tbsp. smooth peanut butter

1 large banana, sliced

Instructions:

1. Preheat the breakfast sandwich maker.
2. Place one slice of bread, already coated with peanut butter, side up inside the bottom tray of the sandwich maker.
3. Top the bread with slices of banana.

4. Place the second piece of bread on top of the banana.

5. Close the sandwich maker and cook for 4 to 5 minutes until heated through.

6. Carefully open the sandwich maker and enjoy your sandwich.

Mediterranean English Muffin

Serves 1

Prep Time: 5 minutes

Cook Time: 5 minutes

Nutritional Value: 340 calories, 31g carbs, 17g fat, 12g protein

Ingredients:

1 English muffin, sliced

1 tsp. olive oil

Salt and pepper to taste

1 ounce feta cheese crumbled

1 roasted red pepper in oil, drained

1 slice tomato

1 tbsp. basil pesto

1 large egg

Instructions:

1. Preheat the breakfast sandwich maker.
2. Place half of the English muffin, cut-side up, inside the bottom tray of the sandwich maker.
3. Brush the English muffin with the olive oil and sprinkle with salt and pepper.
4. Top the muffin with the crumbled feta, roasted red pepper and tomato.
5. Slide the egg tray into place and crack the egg into it. Use a fork to stir the egg, just breaking the yolk.
6. Place the second half of the English muffin on top of the egg.
7. Close the sandwich maker and cook for 4 to 5 minutes until the egg is cooked through.

8. Carefully rotate the egg tray out of the sandwich maker then open the sandwich maker.

9. Remove the top English muffin and brush with basil pesto.

10. Replace the English muffin and enjoy your sandwich.

Mexican-Style Egg and Beans Sandwich

Serves 1

Prep Time: 5 minutes

Cook Time: 5 minutes

Nutritional Value: 350 calories, 30g carbs, 16g fat, 19g protein

Ingredients:

2 slices whole wheat bread

1 ounce shredded Mexican cheese

2 tbsp. refried beans

1 large egg

1 tbsp. sliced green onion

Instructions:

1. Preheat the breakfast sandwich maker.
2. Place one slice of bread inside the bottom tray of the sandwich maker.

3. Top the bread with the refried beans and cheese.

4. Slide the egg tray into place and crack the egg into it. Use a fork to stir the egg, just breaking the yolk.

5. Sprinkle the green onion over the egg then place the second piece of bread on top of the egg.

6. Close the sandwich maker and cook for 4 to 5 minutes until the egg is cooked through.

7. Carefully rotate the egg tray out of the sandwich maker then open the sandwich maker to enjoy your sandwich.

Vegan Sausage Sandwich

Serves 1

Prep Time: 5 minutes

Cook Time: 5 minutes

Nutritional Value: 280 calories, 41g carbs, 8g fat, 22g protein

Ingredients:

1 vegan English muffin, sliced

1 vegan sausage patty, cooked

1 slice Vegan cheese

1 ounce firm tofu

Pinch garlic powder

Salt and pepper to taste

Instructions:

1. Cut the tofu into a circle and sprinkle it with garlic powder, salt and pepper.
2. Heat the oil in a small skillet and add the tofu. Cook for 2 to 3 minutes on each side until lightly browned.
3. Preheat the breakfast sandwich maker.
4. Place half of the English muffin, cut-side up, inside the bottom tray of the sandwich maker.
5. Top the muffin with the sausage patty, vegan cheese and tofu.
6. Place the second half of the English muffin on top of the tofu.
7. Close the sandwich maker and cook for 4 to 5 minutes until heated through.
8. Carefully open the sandwich maker and enjoy your sandwich.

Portabella and Spinach Croissant

Serves 1

Prep Time: 5 minutes

Cook Time: 5 minutes

Nutritional Value: 345 calories, 25g carbs, 20g fat, 15g protein

Ingredients:

1 croissant, sliced

1 tsp. olive oil

1 cup baby spinach

1 tbsp. grated parmesan cheese

1 clove garlic, minced

1 portabella mushroom cap

Salt and pepper to taste

1 large egg

Instructions:

1. Heat the olive oil in a small skillet over medium heat. Stir in the garlic and cook for 1 minute.

2. Add the spinach and cook for 2 minutes, stirring, until just wilted. Remove from heat and stir in the parmesan cheese.

3. Preheat the breakfast sandwich maker.

4. Place half of the croissant, cut-side up, inside the bottom tray of the sandwich maker.

5. Top the croissant with the spinach mixture and the portabella mushroom cap. Sprinkle the mushroom with salt and pepper to taste.

6. Slide the egg tray into place and crack the egg into it. Use a fork to stir the egg, just breaking the yolk.

7. Place the second half of the croissant on top of the egg.

8. Close the sandwich maker and cook for 4 to 5 minutes until the egg is cooked through.
9. Carefully rotate the egg tray out of the sandwich maker then open the sandwich maker to enjoy your sandwich.

Red Pepper and Goat Cheese Sandwich

Serves 1

Prep Time: 5 minutes

Cook Time: 5 minutes

Nutritional Value: 300 calories, 31g carbs, 10g fat, 17g protein

Ingredients:

2 slices multigrain bread

1 ounce goat cheese

2 slices fresh red pepper

1 slice red onion

Salt and pepper to taste

1 large egg

Instructions:

1. Preheat the breakfast sandwich maker.

2. Place one slice of bread inside the bottom tray of the sandwich maker.

3. Top the bread with the goat cheese, red pepper and red onion. Season with salt and pepper to taste.

4. Slide the egg tray into place and crack the egg into it. Use a fork to stir the egg, just breaking the yolk.

5. Place the second slice of bread on top of the egg.

6. Close the sandwich maker and cook for 4 to 5 minutes until the egg is cooked through.

7. Carefully rotate the egg tray out of the sandwich maker then open the sandwich maker to enjoy your sandwich.

Bagel with Lox Sandwich

Serves 1

Prep Time: 5 minutes

Cook Time: 5 minutes

Nutritional Value: 375 calories, 37g carbs, 15g fat, 25g protein

Ingredients:

1 whole grain bagel, sliced

2 ounces smoked salmon

2 tbsp. cream cheese

1 tsp. minced red onion

1 tsp. minced chives

1 large egg

Instructions:

1. Preheat the breakfast sandwich maker.

2. Place one half of the bagel, cut-side up, inside the bottom tray of the sandwich maker.

3. Top the bagel with smoked salmon.

4. Stir together the cream cheese, red onion and chives then spread over the salmon.

5. Slide the egg tray into place and crack the egg into it. Use a fork to stir the egg, just breaking the yolk.

6. Place the second half of the bagel on top of the egg.

7. Close the sandwich maker and cook for 4 to 5 minutes until the egg is cooked through.

8. Carefully rotate the egg tray out of the sandwich maker then open the sandwich maker to enjoy your sandwich.

Parmesan and Bacon on Whole Wheat

Serves 1

Prep Time: 5 minutes

Cook Time: 5 minutes

Nutritional Value: 370 calories, 25g carbs, 18g fat, 24g protein

Ingredients:

2 slices whole wheat bread

3 slices bacon, cooked

2 tablespoons grated parmesan cheese

1 large egg

Instructions:

1. Preheat the breakfast sandwich maker.
2. Place one piece of bread inside the bottom tray of the sandwich maker.

3. Break the pieces of bacon in half and arrange them on top of the bread.

4. Top the bacon with the grated cheese.

5. Slide the egg tray into place and crack the egg into it. Use a fork to stir the egg, just breaking the yolk.

6. Place the second piece of bread on top of the egg.

7. Close the sandwich maker and cook for 4 to 5 minutes until the egg is cooked through.

8. Carefully rotate the egg tray out of the sandwich maker then open the sandwich maker to enjoy your sandwich.

Chocolate Donut Dessert Sandwich

Serves 1

Prep Time: 5 minutes

Cook Time: 5 minutes

Nutritional Value: 445 calories, 52g carbs, 21g fat, 9g protein

Ingredients:

1 chocolate-frosted glazed donut, sliced in half

2 tbsp. chocolate hazelnut spread

1 ounce cream cheese

½ cup sliced strawberries

Instructions:

1. Divide the two tablespoons chocolate hazelnut spread between the donut halves, spreading it evenly along the cut edges.
2. Preheat the breakfast sandwich maker.
3. Place half of the donut inside the bottom tray of the sandwich maker.
4. Top the donut with cream cheese and strawberries.
5. Place the second half of the donut on top of the strawberries.
6. Close the sandwich maker and cook for 4 to 5 minutes until heated through.
7. Carefully open the sandwich maker and enjoy your sandwich.

Tomato Basil Flatbread

Serves 1

Prep Time: 5 minutes

Cook Time: 5 minutes

Nutritional Value: 475 calories, 26g carbs, 29g fat, 36g protein

Ingredients:

1 small round flatbread

1 tsp. olive oil

Salt and pepper to taste

1 thick slice ripe tomato

4 fresh basil leaves

1 slice fresh mozzarella cheese

1 large egg

Instructions:

1. Preheat the breakfast sandwich maker.
2. Place the round flatbread inside the bottom tray of the sandwich maker.
3. Brush the flatbread with the olive oil and sprinkle with salt and pepper.
4. Top the flatbread with the slice of tomato, basil leaves and mozzarella cheese.
5. Slide the egg tray into place and crack the egg into it. Use a fork to stir the egg, just breaking the yolk. Close the sandwich maker and cook for 4 to 5 minutes until the egg is cooked through
6. Carefully rotate the egg tray out of the sandwich maker then open the sandwich maker to enjoy your sandwich.

Vegetarian Boca Sandwich

Serves 1

Prep Time: 5 minutes

Cook Time: 5 minutes

Nutritional Value: 310 calories, 28g carbs, 11g fat, 27g protein

Ingredients:

1 whole wheat thin sandwich bun, sliced

2 tsp. Dijon mustard

1 Boca burger patty

1 slice Swiss cheese

1 large egg, beaten

1 slice red onion

1 slice tomato

Instructions:

1. Preheat the breakfast sandwich maker.
2. Place half of the sandwich bun, cut-side up, inside the bottom tray of the sandwich maker.
3. Brush the sandwich bun with Dijon mustard.
4. Top the sandwich bun with the Boca burger patty and Swiss cheese.
5. Slide the egg tray into place and pour the beaten egg into it.
6. Place the second half of the sandwich bun on top of the egg.
7. Close the sandwich maker and cook for 4 to 5 minutes until the egg is cooked through.
8. Carefully rotate the egg tray out of the sandwich maker then open the sandwich maker.

9. Remove the top of the sandwich bun and top the sandwich with the red onion and tomato.

10. Replace the sandwich bun top and enjoy your sandwich.

Cheddar Hash Brown Biscuit

Serves 1

Prep Time: 10 minutes

Cook Time: 5 minutes

Nutritional Value: 465 calories, 39g carbs, 28g fat, 16g protein

Ingredients:

1 buttermilk biscuit, sliced

1 frozen hash brown patty

1 slice cheddar cheese

1 large egg

Instructions:

1. Heat the butter in a small skillet over medium heat. Add the hash brown patty and cook for 2 to 3 minutes until lightly browned on the underside.

2. Flip the patty and cook until browned on the other side. Remove from heat.

3. Preheat the breakfast sandwich maker.

4. Place half of the biscuit, cut-side up, inside the bottom tray of the sandwich maker.

5. Top the biscuit with the cooked hash brown patty and cheddar cheese slice.

6. Slide the egg tray into place and crack the egg into it. Use a fork to stir the egg, just breaking the yolk.

7. Place the second half of the biscuit on top of the egg.

8. Close the sandwich maker and cook for 4 to 5 minutes until the egg is cooked through.

9. Carefully rotate the egg tray out of the sandwich maker then open the sandwich maker to enjoy your sandwich.

Conclusion

Hopefully, after reading this book you understand the basics and benefits of using a breakfast sandwich maker! Not only is it fun to use a breakfast sandwich maker, but it is a quick and easy way to create healthy, delicious breakfast options. Don't hesitate to experiment with new recipes and feel free to customize the ones you have.

**Enjoy this book and good luck to you as you
get started on your way road to good
health and well-being!**

Printed in Great Britain
by Amazon

10795071R00071